PICTURE THIS

VOLUME TWO ~ THE '40s, '50s & '60s

HANOVER

TABLE OF CONTENTS

FOREWORD

The Hanover Area Historical Society is pleased to provide a selection from its photography collection representative of Hanover and the area as it was in the 1940's, 50's and 60's. We believe that you will experience many enjoyable nostalgic moments as you flip page after page. This book is different from previous photo publications that the Historical Society has contributed to. It is different because most of us have been present during the 40's through the 60's and these photos reinforce those pleasant memories of a simpler time.

The Society's photography committee has only recently been formed and our first project has been to assist the Evening Sun with this publication. We have collectively committed hundreds of hours to select, arrange and identify the final photos that you will find in the following pages. They were selected from a collection of several thousand photos that you and others in our community have graciously allowed your Historical Society to steward for future generations.

Our committee is committed to learning from the Society's experience with volume I published last year. Therefore in this issue, we have arranged street views in order leading away from the square on each street. You will find more full-page photos as we strived for quality, not quantity. We have also included an index to help you locate photos of a particular subject in both volumes. And you will find a list of corrections and additions which pertain to volume I.

We have tracked down numerous leads to determine the location of former buildings and the identity of individuals. To all those who have assisted us, we again send you our appreciation for your kindness. It is amazing how sharp the minds of our senior citizens are regarding their hometown. They can instantly list in succession the residents and businesses located on any given street fifty years ago.

However, even with all the efforts that have gone into ensuring the accuracy of this publication, we can be sure of only one thing. There are bound to be errors discovered by those more knowledgeable than our committee's combined resources. And for that we sincerely apologize. We ask only that you not keep the discoveries of inaccuracies to yourself. Please, please inform us so that we can set the record straight. Call or write the Historical Society or committee members so that we may correct our information and share it with each and every one of you.

The excitement among our committee members has been contagious as we worked on this project. We thank you for your support and the opportunity to entertain and educate you in this manner. And finally, please consider the Hanover Area Historical Society as a respository for your treasured photos.

Hanover Area Historical Society Photography Committee

Allen Haar, chairperson

Clair Biddle

Geraldine Byers

Louise Hoffacker

Francis Fuhrman

Henry McLin

William Marquet

Mark S. Tome

STREET VIEWS

Hanover's street scenes, for the most part, have under gone some drastic changes over the years. Trees were removed and new species planted. Some building facades changed dramatically, others have basically remained the same.

The photographs in this section recall the days when the roads leading into and out of Hanover met at the circle on Center Square and traffic was regulated by signal lights located in the center of the street on the perimeter of the circle. The Pickett monument, commemorating the town's role in the Civil War battle, was once the centerpiece of the Square and the brick pavement offered a pleasing place to take a Saturday afternoon stroll or sit on a park bench under the shade of maple trees that lined the oval.

The traffic, both pedestrian and vehicular, in downtown Hanover in the 1940s and '50s provide evidence of a period of prosperity in the community. While some commercial venues have created other shopping areas over the years, Hanover's Center Square area remains a hub of activity.

Showing pride in their community and an interest to preserve the past, residents purchased and restored many of Hanover's fine old residences. These old homes serve as a testament to the skill and craftsmanship of a day long past.

Note: All section introductions authored by Bob Marchio of *The Evening Sun.*

Removing trees along the east side of 100 block of Baltimore Street. Borough Manager, Chester Eckbert, had many of the trees cut down along borough streets, upsetting many residents. Photo circa 1957.

CENTER SQUARE - PAGES 6-8

View of Hanover's Center Square facing east in the 1940s.

Southeast corner of Center Square in the late 1940s.

Northeast corner of Center Square in the late 1940s. Cannon Shoes, Myers Drug Store and Columbia Jewelry Company are pictured.

BROADWAY - PAGES 9-16

Aerial view of Hanover, looking out Broadway, circa 1953.

2nd block of Broadway, 1947.

View of southeast Hanover Center Square facing Broadway in the 1940s. The Hanover Hotel in center had a fire in the early 1980s and lost the 4th floor.

Northeast corner of Broadway at Center Square, 1947.

121 Broadway in center building, the Western Union office to the left is 123 Broadway (later became Beanie's Shoe Repair), cira 1940.

119 Broadway, circa 1947. Hahn's Broadway Dry Cleaners on left, Berkheimer's Barber Shop on right.

At right is 127 Broadway, Wentz & Birgensmith Tailors, circa 1940. Later Reader's Cafe. On the left is 129 Broadway, L.W. Cleaver Auto Parts.

136 and 138 Broadway, opposite former Post Office, circa 1947.

140, 142 and 144 Broadway, circa 1947.
140 Broadway was home and office of John
Melsheimer, MD.

144 and 146 Broadway at Locust Street, circa 1947. Good Year Store on right.

Residence of Dr. Samuel Kirkpatrick, at 230 and 232 Broadway in the 1960s. This was formerly the residence, and office on left, of Dr. Floyd Lepperd, MD.

YORK STREET - PAGES 17-24

York Street at Broadway, circa 1949. Left to right, Famous Lunch, Roth & Klunk Fabrics, Doubleday Book Shop, Raymond's Men Shop, Henry J Hoffacker, Dentist, Ernie's (Wolfe) Photography, Menchey Music, Knights of Columbus Hall, Hoffman Studio, and Rainbow Cleaners were some of the businesses on York Street in this era.

Looking down the east side of the 1st block of York Street in the late 1940s. The Trinity Reformed Church steeple is in the background.

View of businesses on the east side, 1st block of York Street in the late 1940s.

26, 28, 30, 32 and 34 York Street, circa 1947. Blind Center Building on extreme left at 26 York Street. Rainbow cleaners on extreme right at 34 York Street. Spangler's Wallpaper was located at 30 York Street.

20 York Street, former YMCA Building, included an indoor swimming pool in rear building, later Lyric Band. The structure was originally built as the Franklin House about 1850.

East side of 200 block of York Street, 1947. Lewis H. Sterner MD was located at 230 York Street, home on left.

Southwest corner of York Street at Walnut Street, 1947. The center building was torn down to widen the street. The building to the left was removed and another building erected.

View of the northeast corner of York and East Middle streets, 1947. Trone's Grocery Store in front building, Lohr's Evangelical United Brethren Church in the background.

200 and 202 York Street at the corner of Middle Street, circa 1947.

BALTIMORE STREET - PAGES 25-27

West side of Baltimore Street at Center Square, 1949. Left to right, Metropolitan Edison, Mau-Dra Soda Fountain, Elks Club, Shear's Cut-Rate Store and J.C. Penney Company.

Businesses on the east side, 1st block of Baltimore Street, 1949. 16 Benn's Men's Store, 18 Anthony's Shoe Store, 20 Richman's Woman's Ware, 22 Fisher Insurance, 24 Western Auto, 26 Haines Shoe Company, 28 Leinhart Brothers, 36 Argio Bros. Produce and 38 Hanover Home Association.

East side of Baltimore Street from Center Square, 1947.

Interior of the L.B. Kirkland residence.

Baltimore Street, east side, third block, 1947. St. Joseph's Church and three homes to the left of the church have been torn down. The home on left was Edward Hutton MD office.

Louis and Margaret Kirkland residence at 312 Balitmore Strcct, circa 1966.

FREDERICK STREET - PAGES 28-31

44-52 Frederick Street, opposite State Theater, circa 1940s. Jacob Sell Home, 3rd from left was torn down June, 1949. This became part of the future Sears & Roebuck site which later became the location of the Borough Office.

East side, 1st block of Frederick Street from Central Hotel to State Theater, 1947. Hanover Cafe at 33 Frederick Street, to the right of Center became Victory Restaurant, Concino's Shoe Repair and Bennett Brothers Grocery.

The north side of Frederick Street from Center Square, 1947. Central Hotel on right, the 2nd building was torn down and McCrory's Store was built. It later became the Adams Hanover Counseling Service. The Victory Restaurant opened in the middle building in 1942.

Side of 58 Frederick Street, taken from rear of Sears' construction site in 1950.

281 Frederick Street, next to the Sinclair Station on left, circa 1940. This house was built in 1933 for John A. Nickey by Luke Rohrbaugh.

Sinclair Gas Station at 285 Frederick Street at Forney Avenue, later location of NAPA Auto Parts, circa 1940.

CARLISLE STREET

Carlisle Street looking from Center Square in the 1960s.

SIDE STREETS & OUT OF TOWN - PAGES 33-35

Emma L. Schue home and grocery store at the northwest corner of Centennial Avenue and Middle Street, 1949.

South side, 1st block of Walnut Street off York Street, 1947. Pictured is Stambaugh Auto Parts.

Corner of Chestnut and Railroad streets, circa 1949. B.M Wentz & Son Building. Formerly Acme Extract and Chemical Company. Saint Mark's Church steeple on Carlisle Street in background.

Rebuilding of Middle Street from Centennial Avenue, circa 1957. Northeast corner of Centennial Avenue and Middle Street. The pictured houses are 33-43 Middle Street.

C. L. Weaver residence at 410 Edgegrove Road in the 1960s. The covered bridge, at right, crossed Conewago Creek. Later owned by Greg and Lydia Mummert.

EDUCATION

Education has always held a major role in the progress of a population. Hanover and the surrounding communities are no different.

Hanover's earliest schools were of a parochial nature, having been founded by Lutheran and Reformed congregations in town. In 1835 a free public school system was established to provide an education for the children of Hanover.

As evidenced in photographs appearing in this section, a number of one-room schools thrived in the surrounding rural communities, providing instruction for those children who had no means or the time for daily travel into town. However, for their secondary education, children attended school in Hanover until the 1960s, when surrounding townships joined forces and established their own school systems.

Danner's School on Hoff Road, near Porters Sideling. Mrs. Maude Eyler, teacher, 1948.

Brodbecks School on Route 516 in Brodbecks, F.M. Trump, teacher, 1946.

Nace's School on Impounding Dam Road, William M. Krebs, teacher, 1947.

Shaffer's School, Paul Snyder, teacher, 1948.

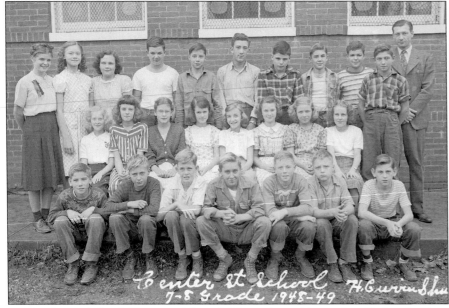

Center Street School, Hanover, 7th and 8th grades, with teacher H. Curvin Shue 1948-1949.

Miller's School, Route 216 outside Brodbecks, William M. Krebs, teacher, 1949.

Center Street School

Center Street School, Hanover, 7th and 8th grades, 1950-51.

Mt. Carmel School, Moulstown Road, M.S. Danner, teacher, 1950.

Center Street School, Hanover, 3rd and 4th grades, Mrs. Eva Garrett, teacher, 1950.

Bandana School, Pleasant Hill, Leon H. Bortner, teacher, 1951.

Fairview School, Baltimore Pike at Fairview Drive, C.L. Snyder, teacher, 1951.

Mathias School, under Long Arm Dam, Mrs. Ruth Crumrine, teacher, 1951.

Bair's School, Mrs. Nace, teacher, 1952.

Pennville School, 7th and 8th grades, 1952.

Hokes School, Glenville Road, D. Baum, teacher, 1952.

Snyder's School on Skyview Drive, Manheim Township. R.B. Bucher was the teacher, 1952.

Wolfgang's School on the corner of Wolfgang Road and Lineboro Road, , Mark A. Wildasin, teacher, 1952.

Pennville School on Frederick Street in Hanover. The 3rd and 4th grades with Mary L. Steger, teacher, 1952.

Stauffer's School, Myrtle E. Kauffman, teacher, 1952.

Brookside School, circa 1950.

SOCIETY

A social life is important to the prosperity of any community.

Counting the social, fraternal, service, veterans and religious affiliations, along with a number of miscellaneous other groups, the community has had more than 200 organizations that contributed to the social scene.

Through private and public functions carried out by their memberships, these organizations strive for a better community.

Let's not forget music. A number of bands, such as the Knights of Phythias Band, and choral groups allowed residents to practice their talents and entertain the multitudes.

The bells on the clock in the steeple of the old St. Mark's Lutheran Church on Carlisle Street sounded for the community. After the congregation built a new church on Charles Street, the part of the old edifice and parsonage were razed. The Sunday school portion of the church on Railroad Street remained standing and served as Hanover's borough hall. The clock now resides in the present St. Mark's Church.

Louis Kirkland, Margaret Kirkland and an unidentified woman (left) at the Hanover Historical Society sign up event, circa 1965.

Pennsylvania Brigade, Uniform Rank Knights of Pythias Band performing at Eichelberger High School, circa 1940.

Lions Club Banquet, McAllister Hotel, circa 1955.

Removal of trees in front of the YWCA on the 1st block of Carlisle Street, 1958.

St. Mark's Lutheran Church at 113 Carlisle Street, circa 1950. Barnitz home on the left, Parsonage on the right. All three buildings were torn down and later became the site of Getty's Service Station.

Conewago Chapel, Edgegrove, Adams County, with frame buildings in foreground, circa 1957.

COMMERCE

Over the years, Hanover residents supported a large number of commercial businesses, which offered the staples for living, and items which made life easier and more luxurious.

Corner grocery stores flourished as well as small eating establishments.

Businesses often opened their doors to allow the community to come in and see how their neighbors practiced their skills in the manufacture of shoes, cigars, gloves, books and numerous other goods.

The Park and State theaters presented the latest in first run movies. Another theater, The Strand, served up the latest in western adventures every Saturday.

Several photographs show construction work on a new Sears building in the first block of Frederick Street. That structure now serves as Hanover's Borough Hall, containing the town's operations center, the Hanover Water Co. offices and police headquarters.

The Kroh's Confectionary store on Center Square was a favorite gathering spot where children could purchase penny candy or a bag of fresh popcorn. Of particular interest in Kroh's was a popcorn machine that contained a small clown, which appeared to be cranking as it popped the delicious treat.

Sinclair Service Station at 407 Baltimore Street at Boundary Avenue, circa 1954. Chronister Beer Distributor at right in the rear, later became Feeser's Beer Distributor.

48 Frederick Street, circa 1940s. Location of Crabbs Detective Agency.

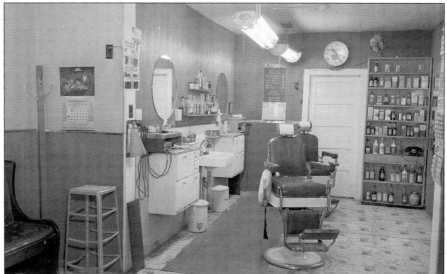

Interior of a Hanover Barber Shop, circa 1940.

Hanover Glove Company display, circa 1940.

Hanover Hardware, Jordan apartment building, Cut-Rate Shoe Store, and the Holland Restaurant (behind utility pole, now Bank of Hanover parking lot), southeast corner of Carlisle and Chestnut streets, circa 1940.

Hanover Shoe Company managers meeting at McAllister Hotel, circa 1942.

Holland Restaurant, 39 Carlisle Street, 1947. It was later torn down and became a parking lot. Photo provided by Clair Biddle.

Interior of The State Theater on Frederick Street after interior remodeling, circa 1960s.

Park Theater, southwest corner of Chestnut and Franklin Streets, later became the location of St. Matthew's Church office, photo circa 1945. It was the Hanover Opera House before it was renamed the Park Theater in 1931.

H.N. Heusner & Son Cigar Company, 228 High Street, circa 1945. Manufacturer of Dan O'Brien Cigars. Later became Tanger's Hardware.

Kessler's Bicycle Shop, 233 Baltimore Street, 1947.

Smith's Drug Store, Broadway, 1947. It was later torn down to widen Railroad Street at Broadway.

The Open Gate BBQ Diner, 1st block of Frederick Street, circa early 1950s.

Baumgardner's Restaurant in the Five Points Building, 19 East Walnut Street, circa 1947.

Concino's Shoe Repair at 37 Frederick Street, 1947.

Terminal Cigar Shop at 17 York Street, 1947.

2nd and 1st blocks of Baltimore Street, 1947.

233 Baltimore Street, Kessler's Bicycles and Gettysburg Autoparts in photo, 1947.

Central Hotel from Frederick Street, 1947.

Eiserman's Wholesale House at 145 Baltimore Street, 1948.

Kinney Shoe Store and Hollanders Auto Supplies, northwest corner of Square under Central Hotel, circa 1948.

Hanover Trust Company and McCrory's 5 & 10 Store at the northwest corner of Square and Carlisle Street in the 1940s.

Trone's Gulf Service Station, which later became Dr. Trans Auto Repair, at 513-517 Broadway, near Stock Street intersection, circa 1948. Building on left is Hanover Motor Company Auto Repairs. Individuals left to right, Morris Trump, Robert E. Trone (son of owner), Clair J. Trone (owner) and Al Brailer.

Sheppard & Myers Building, Center Square and Carlisle Street, circa 1950.

Shirk's Hardware at 40 Broadway, 1948. Smiths Drug Store at right, torn down to widen Railroad Street.

Sherwin-Williams Paint Store and Elmer Wentz Flooring Store on the east side of the first block at 6 Baltimore Street, 1949. The building was badly damaged in a fire during the late 1990s.

Moose Building, Newcomers Cigar Store, and Shirk's Hardware, 1st block on north side of Broadway, circa 1960s.

Interior of Famous Hot Weiner Restaurant, Broadway at York Street, circa 1950.

Myers Brothers Memorials at 261 Third Street, circa 1950. The first Lutheran and Reformed congregations in the Hanover area worshipped in a log church on this site in the first half of the 18th Century. The two congregations later became St. Matthew's Lutheran Church and Emmanuel United Church of Christ within the Borough of Hanover.

Gruver's Grocery Store, corner of West Middle and Baltimore streets, later site of Evening Sun building.

Kinney Shoes display window on the square.

McAllister Hotel back dining Room.

McAllister Hotel staff in banquet room.

Foundation of Sears Store looking from Exchange place against Hanover Glove Building, 1950. St. Matthew's Lutheran Church steeple in the backgroud (later torn down). Crabbs Agency on left.

Blind Center Shop 26 York Street, owned by Cletus Wertz, circa 1950.

Site of Sears Store looking from rear of 1st block of Frederick Street, 1950. This later became the location of Borough Office.

Menchey Music Service display, 18 York Street.

Columbia Jewelry Company looking from Broadway into the square to the J.W. Gitt Building (occupied by J.C. Penney), circa 1952.

Rainbow Cleaners at 34 York Street, circa 1953.

Jesse Crabbs Detective Agency in center section at 50 Frederick Street in the early 1950s. It later became the location of Locksmith & Seamstress. Building at right was formerly John Rupp Furniture Factory. Sears store evident to left.

Baker's and Baker's Little Folks Shop at 35 Broadway in the 1950s.

Tawney's Sinclair Service Station, 283-285 Frederick Street on the corner of North Forney and Frederick streets, circa 1954. Later became NAPA Auto Parts.

Sinclair Service Station employee (possibly Norman Tawney), circa 1954.

Murphy's Cut Rate Store at 31 Baltimore Street, circa 1954.

Shamrock Café at 225 Carlisle Street, circa 1955.

Shamrock Café at 225 Carlisle Street, circa 1955.

Royal Jewelers on the corner of Baltimore Street at the square in the 1950s. Kroh's Confectionary Shop, Hanover Hotel on left. J.C. Penney store on right.

Interior of the Richard McAllister Hotel on the 1st block of York Street, front dining room, circa 1955.

Small's Texaco Service Station, 320 Carlisle Street at Railroad, circa 1956. Later became Bixler's Texaco. Irvin (Houck's) Appliance Store and A&P Grocery Store to the left.

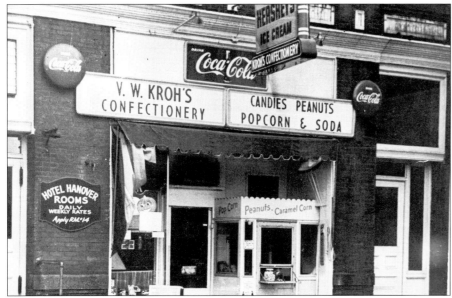

Kroh's Confectionery on the square in the Hotel Hanover Building, circa 1957. The historical society owns the Kroh Popcorn Machine and is in need of photos and funds to restore it.

Elmer E. Wentz Sons flooring store, 955 Carlisle Street in the 1960s.

Murphy's, Bennett Brothers and Paragon Shoes on the corner of Carlisle Street and Center Square, May, 1962.

Steele's Laundry Cleaning Storage Company at 110 High Street in the early 1960s.

Flat Iron building on the corner of East Chestnut and Broadway, circa 1960. The building was torn down to widen Chestnut Street and provide turning radius from Broadway.

Famous Lunch building on the corner of York and Broadway, circa 1965.

INDUSTRY

The pride and dedication among workers fueled the industries of Hanover through the middle of the 20th century.

These laborers supported manufacturers of shoes and of products related to the shoe industry, cigars, wire screening, jute for carpet backing, clothing and a host of other products.

Even during depression years industries in Hanover and surrounding areas attempted to keep jobs for their employees.

The Utz Potato Chip plant built on Carlisle Street in the late 1940s stands as just one symbol of a thriving snack food industry.

Supplementing the town's heavy industry was a number of skilled and professional support businesses such as plumbers, machinists, mechanics, etc.

Middleburg Sewing Factory on Linden Avenue.

Middleburg Sewing Factory on Linden Avenue.

Middleburg Sewing Factory on Linden Avenue.

C.E. Bechtel Heating and Electric Company, 1st block of Frederick Street, circa 1940.

Hearn Bottling Works at the 1400 block of Broadway, circa 1945. It closed in 1960 and became Delone Beverage Company, a beer distributor.

Coulson Heel Company, 301 Poplar Street, later became the location of CH Reed.

Hanover Cordage Company, East Chestnut Street, circa 1945. It was torn down in the 1990s and became the site of Capitol Storage.

Inside the Hanover Shoe Company, Carlisle Street, October, 1960. Windows facing railroad track.

Beaudin Shoe Company on Factory Street, circa 1946.

Utz Potato Chip Factory, Clearview Road at Carlisle Street in the 1960s.

Hanover Glove Company employees at the Hotel New Yorker, 1948. Front row, left to right, Unidentified, Mrs. Reiff. Second row, Horace Burg, Maurice Reiff, Customer, Jack Fox, and unknown. The company was bought by the Gitt Family from the Wolf Buckskin Glove Company in 1885 and sold to the Fairfield Glove Company, Fairfield, Iowa in 1963.

Fitz Water Wheel, manufactured in Hanover. Location of this installation is not known.

PUBLIC SERVICE

Hanover's public servants have always been dedicated to maintaining a peaceful and safe community.

Hanover General Hospital opened in 1926. Local entrepreneurs and philanthropists, H. D. Sheppard and C.N. Myers, owners of the Hanover Shoe Co., financed the hospital's construction and provided an endowment for its maintenance.

In earlier days individual physicians maintained the community's health the best they could. Medicine was often supplemented by a family's traditional home remedy.

The need for fire protection was realized soon after Hanover's founding. The Hanover Fire Department maintains its first pieces of fire apparatus in a museum near the Hanover Fire Co. No.1 station on North Franklin Street. Included is a Silsby steam engine placed in service in 1882.

A high constable was the first to maintain law and order. Officer Frank Mulhorn, pictured in this section, rides a three-wheeled Harley-Davidson motorcycle once used by the Hanover Police Department for street patrol, mostly in the downtown area.

The YWCA's Garden Club has helped beautify the Center Square area with the planting of seasonal flowers and plants.

Hanover General Hospital at Highland Avenue and Charles Street in the 1960s.

Police Officer, Frank Mulhorn, at 104 Baltimore Street in front of Al's Barber Shop (later Rohrbaugh's Barber Shop) and Kleffel's Clothing Store, 1949.

Landscaping Hanover's Center Square, with the horse facing out Frederick Street, 1954.

Rear addition to Post Office, Broadway and Locust Street, 1956.

Breaking ground for the Hanover Armory, Clearview Road, west side of Carlisle Street in background, circa 1958.

Eagle Fire Company, East Hanover Street, circa 1960. Left to right, Lloyd (Hessy) Ripka, Richard Scheivert, Earl Bortner, Holman L. (Pete) Lemmon, and the mascot, Smokey. Smokey served the fire department from 1958-1968.

Hanover Borough Council, 1960. Front left to right, JC Heltebridle, Donald W. Resh, Burnell Stambaugh, C.E. Bechtel, Gerald E. Wertman. Back row, Harry N. Bange, J.W. McCullough, Horace Thoman, Elizabeth Ackerman, Joseph O'Brien, Donald Albright, Paul Worcester, Lester M. Jacobs, Raymond A. Harding.

RECREATION & CELEBRATION

People proudly step forward at any chance to wave the Red, White and Blue. The return of men and women who served during two World Wars was cause for celebration. A photo in this section shows the welcome presented to World War II veterans.

Started after World War I, the community's Memorial Day celebration has been a tradition. Veterans and patriotic groups march to Mt. Olivet Cemetery on Baltimore Street for a service of remembrance. Accompanying veterans are high school and other musical groups.

Various forms of recreation were available in the 40s through the 60s. Biddle's park off Stock Street was a year around delight for children from various neighborhoods and there was always time for a friendly game of baseball or softball. Hanover Borough, with cooperation from the Hanover Public School District, also offered a summer recreation program at various school and community playgrounds.

The roller coaster at Forest Park, an amusement park located on Baltimore Street adjacent to Mt. Olivet Cemetery, provided exciting thrills. The coaster was the centerpiece of a number of other amusement rides that entertained park patrons. The park also maintained a popular roller skating rink and bandstand in which numerous bands and musical groups, both local and national, performed.

School children were always eager to participate in decorating the windows of downtown businesses sponsored by the Hanover Jaycees as part of their annual community Halloween celebration.

V.F.W. Drum and Bugle Corps at Hanover Savings Fund Society on 1st block of Carlisle Street, 1942.

Lyric Band during a 1940s concert at State Theater on Frederick Street.

Autokraft Box Corporation annual picnic, June 24, 1944. Autokraft was located on Commerce Street.

Memorial Day Parade marching south on Baltimore Street at the entrance to Mt. Olivet Cemetary in the 1940s.

The Color Guard participates in a 1940s Memorial Day parade marching south on Baltimore Street at Mt. Olivet Cemetary.

A group of men enjoying the beautiful view at Dick's Dam, Conewago Creek.

Weathervane Furniture Company float in a 1940s parade. Weathervane Furniture was at 600 Elm Avenue at railroad track from about 1950 to about 1983.

Hanover throws a Welcome Home party for WWII soldiers, at Center Square, September 2, 1946.

Forest Park on Baltimore Street, circa 1950s. Note S&H Green Stamp sign.

Forest Park, Baltimore Street past Mt. Olivet Cemetery, circa 1960s.

Forest Park, with Baltimore Street in the foreground, circa 1960s.

Forest Park, circa 1955. Baltimore Street in background. Buses transported customers from Baltimore. The remains of amusement park ride foundations are evident.

Forest Park, Baltimore Street, circa 1955. The park operated until 1966 when a shopping center was built.

Forest Park on Baltimore Street, September, 1946.

The "Heyday" ride at Forest Park, Baltimore Street, circa 1955.

A group of folks enjoying a ride at Forest Park, Baltimore Street, circa 1960.

Shooting gallery at Forest Park, Baltimore Street, circa 1955.

Gospel Band at Biddle's Green Pine Park, circa 1950. The park was built by Mr. A.M. Biddle at Penn and George Street, off Broadway. Mr. Biddle had a shoe shine business and devoted much of his income and efforts to the park.

Possibly on the Conewago Creek.

Hanover Halloween window painting contest in the 1950s. J.C. Penney store on the southwest corner of Center Square on Baltimore Street.

Hanover Halloween window painting contest on the northeast corner of Center Square in the 1950s.

Hanover Halloween window painting contest in the 1950s. McAllister Hotel on York Street.

Hanover Halloween window painting contest in the 1950s. J.C. Penney on southwest corner of Center Square.

Bowling in the 1950s. Republican Club on West side of 1st Block of Carlisle Street. Left to right, Bill Lutter, Bob Weller, Nelson Lapham, Unknown, Charlie Criswell, Dick Pentz.

Bicentennial parade.

Bicentennial parade..

Band concert on the northeast corner of Square at Carlisle Street in the 1960s.

"Paint Out" at Flea Market Day, People's Bank on southwest corner of Square, 1966.

Clausen Flag collection displayed on Center Square looking out Broadway, 1966. The Historical Society is now the flag collection caretaker. The collection is available for educational purposes.

Veterans and town officials lead the Memorial Day Parade on Carlisle Street as it approaches Center Square, 1966.

German Band at Flea Market Day, 1966. Center Square with Bon Ton Store at Carlisle Street.

Hanover High School band during Flea Market Day, 1966.

Memorial Day parade on the southeast corner of Center Square, 1966. Portion of Clausen flag collection pictured.

Moose Band at Wirt Park during Flea Market Day, 1966.

Hanover High School band marching south on Carlisle Street into Center Square, Memorial Day parade, 1966.

Hanover Market on Chestnut Street during Flea Market Day, 1966.

CORRECTIONS & ADDITIONS TO VOLUME I

Page	Location	Correction
5		**Corner of Broadway and <u>Locust</u>** Street
10	Bottom Right	Circa **<u>1895</u>**
16		**<u>Wirt</u>**
18		**<u>Joshua</u>** Flickinger
21		**<u>Peoples Bank</u>**
37	Right	Hanover Savings **<u>Fund Society</u>** Bank
44	Top Left	Circa **<u>1950</u>**
45	Right	Circa **<u>1950</u>**
48		Located on corner of Frederick Street and Forney Avenue
50		Located in alley behind 1st block of Frederick Street
50-52		These are installations of water wheels made by Fitz Water Wheel Co.
54	Bottom Left	On Frederick Street
55	Bottom Left & Right	Both photos are of wire processing probably at Hanover Wire Cloth Co.
58	Top Left	**<u>Davidson H & C Company</u>** employees around **<u>1950</u>** in new office at 425 Broadway with Jacob, Chester and Annie Bechtel
58	Top Right	Rear of Carlisle Street near N. Franklin Street
60		**<u>St. Paul's Lutheran Church, York Street</u>**
67	Bottom	**<u>Great Conewago Presbyterian Church in Hunterstown</u>**
70	Bottom Left	On York Street
72	Both Top	Y<u>W</u>CA
74		Wadsworth brothers from Syracuse, NY, circa **<u>1920</u>**, not certain if this is a Hanover scene
77	Left	**<u>H.D.</u>** Sheppard and **<u>C.N.</u>** Myers
80	Top Right	Original Walnut Street School which was town down in 1904 and subsequently replaced with the yellow brick school which later became apartments.
81		**<u>Hanover</u>** High School class in front of A. W. Eichelberger Building
84		**<u>Central Catholic</u>** High School, McSherrystown
89	Top Left	**<u>York</u>** Trolley on Broadway in Hanover
90	Bottom Left	**<u>1903</u>**
105	Bottom Left	**<u>Norm Keeney</u>**, Hanover **<u>Police</u>** chief
124	Right	**<u>Center Electric Theater,</u>** a nickelodeon owned from 1907-1909 by Milton W. Sheaffer, in center of entrance way, and located in Hotel O'Bold (now Hufnagle's Hanover Hotel) on **<u>Center Square,</u>** and closed June 1909. Circa **<u>1908.</u>**
125	Bottom Left	Located in Opera House building
126	Top Right	Circa **<u>1935</u>**

I hope you have enjoyed another trip down "Memory Lane" with the most recent edition of *Picture This: Hanover*. The eras represented in this newest pictorial history cover decades that many us remember well and fondly from the beehive of activity at the Hanover Shoe Factory to the square with its grassy traffic circle. I'm sure this volume has brought back many wonderful memories. I know that it has for me, including dropping my daughters off downtown to browse in the "5 & Dime" stores and then take in a matinee at the Hanover Theater on Frederick Street.

While leafing through the pages, you probably saw more clearly the shape of today's Hanover and possibly caught a glimpse of what our future will hold.

Because I and members of my family remember these years so well, we were very happy to again sponsor *Picture This: Hanover*.

–The Honorable Mayor Margret F. Hormel

INDEX OF NAMES & PLACES FOR VOLUMES I & II

INDEX OF STREET NAMES FOR VOLUMES I & II